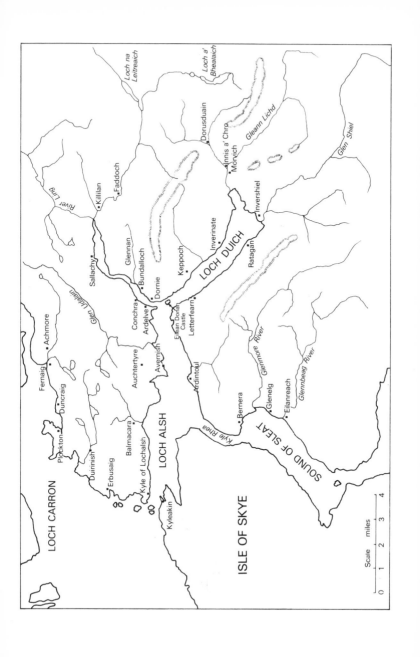

PERSONAL ARMS OF MACRAE OF INVERINATE

PERSONAL ARMS OF MACRAE OF CONCHRA

THE CLAN MACRAE

JOHNSTON'S CLAN HISTORIES

THE CLAN CAMERON. BY C.I. FRASER OF REELIG, *Sometime Albany Herald*.

THE CLAN CAMPBELL. BY ANDREW MCKERRAL, C.I.E.

THE CLAN DONALD. (Macdonald, Macdonell, Macalister). BY I.F. GRANT, LL.D.

THE FERGUSSONS. BY SIR JAMES FERGUSSON OF KILKERRAN, BT.

THE CLAN FRASER OF LOVAT. BY C.I. FRASER OF REELIG, *Sometime Albany Herald*.

THE CLAN GORDON. BY JEAN DUNLOP, PH.D.

THE GRAHAMS. BY JOHN STEWART OF ARDVORLICH.

THE CLAN GRANT. BY I.F. GRANT, LL.D.

THE KENNEDYS. BY SIR JAMES FERGUSSON OF KILKERRAN, BT.

THE CLAN MACGREGOR. BY W.R. KERMACK.

THE CLAN MACKAY. BY MARGARET O. MACDOUGALL.

THE CLAN MACKENZIE. BY JEAN DUNLOP, PH.D.

THE CLAN MACKINTOSH. BY JEAN DUNLOP, PH.D.

THE CLAN MACLEAN. BY JOHN MACKECHNIE.

THE CLAN MACLEOD. BY I.F. GRANT, LL.D.

THE CLAN MACRAE. BY DONALD MACRAE.

THE CLAN MORRISON. BY ALICK MORRISON.

THE CLAN MUNRO. BY C.I. FRASER OF REELIG, *Sometime Albany Herald*.

THE ROBERTSONS. BY SIR IAIN MONCREIFFE OF THAT ILK, BT. *Albany Herald*.

THE CLAN ROSS. BY DONALD MACKINNON, D.LITT.

THE SCOTTS. BY JEAN DUNLOP, PH.D.

THE STEWARTS. BY JOHN STEWART OF ARDVORLICH.

THE CLAN MACRAE

The Scattered Children of Kintail

BY

DONALD MACRAE

JOHNSTON & BACON
(A DIVISION OF GEOFFREY CHAPMAN LTD.)
EDINBURGH AND LONDON

First Published 1970
SBN 7179 4547 2
© *Geoffrey Chapman Ltd.*

To

FLORA BURDETTE TAYLOR
San Antonio, Texas

And

AGNES MACRAE MORTON
Linville, North Carolina

This book is set in Press Roman 11pt (IBM) by
Claire Graphics London SW19

PRINTED IN GREAT BRITAIN BY
LOWE AND BRYDONE (PRINTERS) LTD., LONDON

THE CLAN MACRAE
The Scattered Children of Kintail

I

The name MacRae is a personal one and not a patronymic like MacDonald. It originated quite independently in various places in Ireland and Scotland from an early date and was given to individuals who were in no way connected with each other. In Gaelic and Old Irish, *Mac-Rath* literally means 'son of prosperity' or 'divine grace' and the name appears in Scotland as early as the reign of Malcolm IV (1141-1165), when a certain MacRaith de Ospitali witnessed the gift of a church to the canons of Holyrood. The name first appears as a surname in the North of Scotland in an agreement made at Inverness in 1386 between the Bishop of Moray and the Wolf of Badenoch. This document refers to land in Rothiemurchus, Inverness-shire which was at one time occupied by a certain Cristinus MacRath. From that date, the name is frequently met with as a surname in various parts of Scotland, particularly in the Shires of Ross, Perth, Ayr and Dumfries.

The little that is known of the early history and origin of the MacRaes of Kintail with which this book deals is based on a manuscript written originally by the Rev. John MacRa of Dingwall, who died in 1704 and later transcribed by Farquhar MacRa, (Camden, South Carolina, 1870). According to this document, the MacRaes who settled in Kintail are said to have lived on the lands of Lovat, near the southern shore of the Beauly Firth where there was a site called *Larach tigh MhicRath* (the site of MacRae's house). It is also said that a stone was erected at the door of Lovat's castle which read:

'Fhad 'sa bhitheas Frisealach a stigh, na bitheadh MacRath a muigh'.

'As long as a Fraser lives within, let not a MacRae remain without'.

It is difficult to determine why the MacRaes left the Clunes district but it is reasonable to suppose that Lovat's own kindred was increasing and that the land was required by them. The result was that, according to tradition three of the sons of the MacRae of Clunes left the district. One settled at Brahan, near Dingwall, where there was a piece of land named *Cnoc MhicRath* (the hill of MacRae) and a well called *Tobair Mhicrath* (MacRae's well). Another son went to Argyllshire, while the third son is said to have gone to Kintail, probably in the first half of the fourteenth century, before the MacKenzies were granted a charter for their lands in Kintail. Having settled in Kintail, MacRae married a MacBeolan or Gillanders, a kinswoman of the Earls of Ross by whom Kintail was held before it fell into the hands of the MacKenzies. When the MacKenzies did become Barons of Kintail they expected loyal and faithful support from the MacRaes and this they obtained, through the centuries, in full measure. The MacRaes formed the bodyguard of the Chief of Kintail, while the MacLennans, who occupied part of Kintail at that time became the standard bearers. The MacRaes were so instrumental in raising the Barony of Kintail to such an important position in the history of the Highlands that they were known as 'MacKenzie's shirt of mail'. From early times it was the privilege of the

MacRaes to bear the dead bodies of Barons of Kintail and later the Lords of Seaforth to their place of burial. The last occasion this happened was when the Hon. Mrs. Stewart-MacKenzie, daughter of the last Lord Seaforth was buried in 1862. Her coffin was borne out of Brahan Castle by MacRaes only.

According to the Rev. John MacRa, the founder of the MacRaes of Kintail was *Fionnla Dubh MacGillechriosd* (Black Finlay, son of Christopher), a grandson of the MacRae who came from Clunes. Black Finlay lived at the same time as Murdo MacKenzie, 5th Chief of Kintail who died in 1416.

After the Earldom of Ross was annexed to the crown from the MacDonalds of the Isles in 1476, the Mac-Kenzies rose to great power and influence in the North. In 1491 an organised insurrection took place under the leadership of Alexander MacDonald of Lochalsh, a natural son of Celestine, son of the Lord of the Isles. Alexander assumed the title of Earl of Ross, invaded the mainland to substantiate his claim and with the help of the Clan Chattan captured Inverness. On his return to the west he was assisted by the Clan Cameron and ravaged the land of the MacKenzies. Near Strathpeffer, at a place afterwards called *Blar na Pairc* (The Battlefield of the Park), MacDonald was defeated by the Kintail men. In the battle there was one, Duncan MacRae, a henchman of MacKenzie, who slew so many of the enemy that he was given the name, Big Duncan of the Battleaxe. Duncan's prowess is commemorated in the well known bagpipe tunes: *Spaidsearachd MhicRath* The MacRae's March) and *Blar na Pairc* (The Battle of the Park).

According to J.H. Dixon, who wrote *Gairloch, its Records, Traditions & Inhabitants*, the MacRaes were

largely instrumental in establishing the MacKenzies in
control of that area. About 1480, Allan MacLeod, laird
of Gairloch, with his two sons was murdered by his
brothers. MacLeod's wife was a sister of Hector Mac-
Kenzie of Kintail and he obtained a commission from
King James IV in 1494 for the subjugation of the
MacLeods. When this was accomplished with the assistance of the MacRaes, MacKenzie received a grant of
Gairloch by charter from the crown.

When Donald (Gruamach) MacDonald of Sleat attacked Eilean Donan in 1539, another Duncan MacRae, who
was an accomplished archer mortally wounded Donald
with a barbed arrow. After the death of their leader, the
MacDonalds retired and the castle was saved. As a
reward for this and other aid rendered to the Lords of
Kintail, Duncan was granted the lands of Inverinate
about 1557. These lands remained in the family for over
two hundred years. The descendants of Duncan were
known locally as the 'Fair MacRaes' as opposed to his
brother Farquhar's family who were called the 'Black
MacRaes'.

After Lord Kintail wrested the Island of Lewis from
the Fife Adventurers and the MacLeods, he sent the
Rev. Farquhar MacRae to the island to restore Christian
rites to the people. The Rev. Farquhar who was born in
Eilean Donan in 1580 was first appointed vicar of
Gairloch in 1608 and after his return from Lewis he
became vicar of Kintail. While he served in this capacity
he lived in Eilean Donan and acted as tutor to the sons
of Seaforth and neighbouring lairds. During the time of
Cromwell, when General Monk's army invaded Kintail
in 1654, they took away over three hundred of the
Rev. Farquhar's cattle but he, a staunch Royalist and
Episcopalian, refused to claim compensation when

MACRAE, DRESS

EILEAN DONAN CASTLE

Charles II was restored in 1660. His grandson, *Donnachadh nan Pios* (Duncan of the silver cups), was the compiler of the Fernaig Manuscript (circa 1693) which is a valuable contribution to the study of the earlier language of the Highlands. Duncan, who studied at Edinburgh University had, before settling down in Kintail travelled widely on the Continent. His manuscript contains poems written by himself and by other writers of the age and these give an indication of the contemporary religious and political turmoils.

I I

In the fifteenth century the Chiefs of Kintail moved eastward from Eilean Donan and lived at Kinellan, near Strathpeffer. After Colin MacKenzie, 2nd Lord Kintail was created Earl of Seaforth by King James VI in 1623, he built Brahan Castle and made it his residence. When MacKenzie left Kintail he took with him a large number of MacLennans and the lands of Kintail were left mainly in the hands of the MacRaes. This is borne out by the fact that when the Forfeited Estates Commission carried out their investigation in Kintail after 1718, they found that out of seventy tenants on the Seaforth estates in Kintail, there were two families of MacLennans while there were fifty families with the surname MacRae.

During the long period of religious and civil wars which preceded and followed the Revolution of 1688, the MacRaes under Seaforth supported the Episcopalian Church and the Stuarts, except when they fought rather ingloriously against Montrose at the Battle of Auldearn, near Forres in 1645. At the Battle of Sheriffmuir in 1715, Seaforth joined Mar who was in command of the Jacobite forces and a writer of the time states that the

Mathesons of Lochalsh and the MacRaes of Kintail, who were on the left flank of Mar's army were the only part of Seaforth's forces who behaved with valour. When the rest ran away the MacRaes and Mathesons held their ground until a large number of them were left dead on the field. Tradition relates that this battle made fifty-eight widows in Kintail. To commemorate the clan's gallant stand a memorial cairn was erected at the instance of the Clan MacRae Society on the site of the battlefield, and unveiled on 23rd September, 1922. Among the MacRaes who fought in the battle there was a young man who was seriously wounded and taken to a neighbouring farm house where he was nursed until he recovered. Instead of returning to Kintail, he married the daughter of the farmer, and one of his descendants was the Rev. David MacRae who was a prominent divine and the author of numerous books and pamphlets, including *The Americans at Home* which has recently been reprinted in the U.S.A. In this book he records interviews he had with Longfellow, Emerson, Generals Grant and Lee and many others.

Because he had taken part in the Rebellion of 1715, Seaforth forfeited his titles and estates and escaped to France. During his absence his estates in Wester Ross were controlled by his factor Colonel Donald Murchison of Lochalsh who, with an army of Kintail men, on several occasions prevented government forces from entering Kintail to collect rents. Murchison, however, had the rents collected and, often at great personal risk, arranged for the money to be sent to Seaforth.

In 1719, Seaforth returned to Kintail with the Earl Marischal, the Marquis of Tullibardine and three hundred Spanish troops. They were defeated by the Hanoverians, led by General Wightman at the Battle of Glenshiel.

During the battle, Seaforth was wounded but he, with the principal officers, succeeded in escaping to the Continent. The local people, however, suffered because General Wightman spent several days in Kintail burning the houses of the inhabitants. As a result of this abortive rising Eilean Donan Castle, of which the MacRaes were Constables, was blown up and remained a ruin until it was restored in 1932 by Colonel John MacRae-Gilstrap whose ancestor had, in 1677 received a wadset (i.e. a deed from a debtor to a creditor assigning the rents of land until the debt was paid) of the lands of Conchra in Lochalsh. Today the estate of Conchra is owned by the Colonel's daughter, Miss Dorothy MacRae, and the Castle of Eilean Donan is the property of his grandson, John MacRae.

Although the MacRaes were not out in the Forty-Five Rebellion as a clan, there were several members serving with other fighting units for the Stuarts. According to Bishop Forbes in *The Lyon in Mourning* Vol. 1. p.p. 97-99, a Captain MacRaw accompanied the Prince in Glenkingie during July and August, 1746. After the Battle of Culloden, Murdoch MacRaw, a Kintail man was arrested in or near Fort Augustus, taken to Inverness on 10th May, 1746 where, within the hour, he was hanged at the cross on an apple tree. The only thing the Hanoverians alleged against him was that he was a spy, which he positively denied. According to legend, the leaves of the tree withered and no apples grew on it again. A quotation from *Antiquarian Notes* (1865) by Charles Fraser-MacKintosh refers to the incident.

> 'No wonder, when impiety
> At once attacked the tree and me
> When void of reason, right and law
> Most innocently hanged MacRae'.

In 1771; Kenneth MacKenzie who had not been involved in the Rebellion of 1745, regained the title of Earl of Seaforth and when the American troubles began in 1775, Kenneth, to show his gratitude to George III, offered to raise a regiment in his territory. In this, the 78th Regiment, as the Seaforths were first called, there were so many MacRaes enlisted that they were given the name 'The Wild MacRaes'. In August 1778, the Seaforths marched to Leith, for embarkation to India. It was here that a 'mutiny' of the regiment occurred which is known as 'The Affair of the MacRaes'. The men mutinied because they were under the impression that the government was selling them to the East India Company. The difficulty was however amicably solved without loss of life and half the regiment was sent to Guernsey and half to Jersey as a defence against the French. In 1781 both divisions assembled at Portsmouth and from there they were shipped to India. After nearly two centuries of fighting with distinction in many theatres of war, the Seaforths are today joined with the Camerons and are called the Queen's Own Highlanders. But the MacRaes did not confine themselves to enlisting in the Seaforths. Many joined other regiments. One of these was Colonel Sir John MacRae of Ardintoul, Glenshiel, who joined the Camerons, fought with Sir John Moore at Corunna in 1809 and served later in India. He died in 1847 and was buried in *Clachan Duich* cemetery in Kintail. A plain iron cross on the wall of the old ruined church there marks his last resting place.

III

The old parish of Kintail, which included Glensheil until it was made into a separate parish by the Lords

Commissioners of Teinds in 1726, is situated in the south-west of the County of Ross. Kintail, which in Gaelic means 'the head of the salt water', is the clan country of the MacRaes. Of this wild mountainous country a writer of an earlier century wrote: 'From whatever quarter Kintail is entered, whether by sea from the west or by land from the east, a scene gradually unfolds itself which is impossible to describe. Mountains of immense magnitude grouped together in the sublimest manner, with wood and water, scars and bens intermingled, present a prospect seldom surpassed in wild beauty and equally interesting and astounding in the storms of winter and in the calm serenity of summer'. From the sea coast the country opens up into the three large valleys of Glenelchaig, Glenlic and Glenshiel. These glens surrounded by steep mountains are for most of the year covered with grass from base to summit. The richness of the pasture was the main reason why in the pastoral age of the Highlands, Kintail was noted for its black cattle. The arable land in the glens is, however, in most places infertile and the heavy rainfall makes the securing of crops difficult. In spite of these drawbacks, the period preceding and following the rebellion of 1745 seems to have been an era when the inhabitants of Kintail enjoyed a certain measure of prosperity and it was often referred to as a kind of golden age. It is, according to the Statistical Accounts, likely that the people during this period, possessed in a high degree the substantial comforts of life. Secluded by their inaccessible position from the turmoils of the times, enjoying security of life and property and holding their lands on such terms as admitted of their consuming among themselves a large proportion of their produce, they passed their days in peace and comparative comfort.

The country was, at this period, exclusively stocked with black cattle and the flesh of these together with dairy produce, oatcakes and salmon constituted their staple diet. The era of prosperity in Kintail, however, was short lived. With the defeat at Culloden it can be said that conditions altered with the changed relationship between Seaforth and his tenants. The basis of land tenure before 1746 was the value of the tenant as a soldier and the land which Seaforth held in trust for his people was parcelled out to his principal supporters or tacksmen. Payment of rents was in kind or services. After the middle of the eighteenth century the heads of the clans needed paying tenants and not trains of dependents who would fight for them and since chiefs now lived in the cities outside the clan country, they increased rents in order to keep up their positions as 'Highland gentlemen'. As a result the people felt insecure as they depended more and more on the goodwill of lairds, factors and tacksmen. Some tacksmen could not tolerate squeezing the last farthing out of their tenants and left Scotland for the American Colonies taking their tenants with them. The Society for the Propagation of Christian Knowledge stated: 'In the year 1772 no less than sixteen vessels full of emigrants sailed from the western part of Inverness and Ross, containing, it is supposed 6,400 souls and carrying with them at least £38,000 sterling'. Robert Chambers (1802-1871) writing about the MacRaes stated: 'This clan is said to be the most unmixed in the Highlands, a circumstance which seems to be attended with quite a contrary effect from what might have been expected, the MacRaes being the handsomest and most athletic men beyond the Grampians'. This comment which may have been true nearly two hundred years ago is not the case today, for in the intervening years the country has been denuded of its inhabitants and the MacRaes of Kintail are scattered throughout the world. Of the 450 members of the clan who lost their lives in the 1914-1918 war, not more than a dozen came from the Kintail district! Today there are more persons with the surname MacRae listed in the telephone directory of Vancouver than there are in the whole of Kintail and Glenshiel. Mass emigrations between 1770 and 1780 and evictions over a period of fifty years scattered the clan to U.S.A., Canada, Australia and New Zealand. It is to these 'Scattered Children of Kintail' that we must now turn our attention, for theirs is a story of human endurance, success and failure. And in their wanderings they have given the name MacRae to towns, villages and districts in Georgia, Arkansas and Montana in the United States, to a district in Yukon, Canada, to a mountain in Western Australia and to Macraes Flat, North Otago, New Zealand. [1] Although the Rev. Christopher MacRae is known to have gone before the year 1765 to Virginia where his descendants still live, it was not until after 1770 that large numbers of the clan emigrated from Kintail to North Carolina. John Beaton or Bethune, a son of the minister of Glenshiel had left for the colony earlier and had sent back letters with glowing descriptions of the new land and its prospects. One of the persons influenced by these reports was John MacRae *(Ian MacMhurachaidh),* the Kintail bard, who in songs and poems exhorted his clansmen to emigrate to this land where game and fish could be had in abundance. Although in relatively comfortable circumstances, he resolved to emigrate, and with a contingent of Kintail people, set

1   *Meade's 'Old Churches and Families of Virginia'.*

sail for Carolina. Soon after their arrival, the American War of Independence broke out and the bard at once joined the British forces and took part in the defence of what he considered to be the rights of his native land. It is highly probable that the poet had to swear an oath of loyalty to King George III, for according to Duane Meyer in *Highland Scots in North Carolina,* colonists who obtained land had on arrival to swear 'firm and unalterable loyalty and attachment to the King'. In one of his best songs, written while he served as a soldier in the King's army, he compares his wretched position then with his former free and happy life in Kintail. The poor bard bitterly regretted that he had ever left his homeland and drew a vivid contrast between his miserable condition in the forests of America and the jovial days of his youth. Before the end of the war he was taken prisoner and confined in a wretched dungeon in the forest where he died. In his last poem, a lament, he still looked forward with hope to the arrival of Cornwallis, who, in 1781 surrendered at Yorktown. *'Ach na-n tigeadh Cornwallis 's mise d'fhalbhadh ro-dheonach leis'.* 'But if Cornwallis should come, gladly would I go with him'. Among those who accompanied the poet, there was another John MacRae who lost his arm in the war. He eventually succeeded in making his way back to Kintail, and brought back with him about a dozen of the bard's compositions. But North Carolina's first poet is buried somewhere in the eastern part of the 'Tar Heel' State in an unknown, forgotten grave. It has recently been suggested that a cairn be erected to his memory on MacRae Meadows, Linville or at the village of Invershiel in North Carolina.

I V

One of several Duncan MacRaes who left Kintail in 1774 settled in North Carolina and married an Ann Cameron. Their son John became editor of a local newspaper and he numbered among his friends many men famous in American history, among them General Lafayette whom he entertained in his home and accompanied through North Carolina on his American tour in 1825. John's son, Duncan Kirkland MacRae (1820-1888) who was born at Fayetteville (then Campbelltown) N.C. became a lawyer and was elected to the legislature of N.C. in 1842. Between 1853 and 1857 he became American consul in Paris but on the outbreak of the Civil War he was appointed Colonel of the 5th N.C. Regiment. After he was wounded at Williamsburg and again at Sharpsburg, he was sent on a mission to Europe to find a market for Southern cotton and arrange for supplies. On his return, he edited a newspaper called the *Confederate* at Raleigh (1864-65) to encourage Southern morale.

One man who helped in the development of the western region of North Carolina, was Hugh MacRae (1865-1950), a descendant of Roderick MacRae who left Kintail in 1774. Hugh's grandfather, General Alexander MacRae, organised an artillery battalion for coastal defence during the Civil War (1861-1865), while Hugh's father, Donald, put the output of his iron mills at the disposal of the Confederate forces during the war. Hugh, himself, who graduated as an engineer from the Massachusetts Institute of Technology in Boston, helped to develop the mineral assets of the state of N.C. and

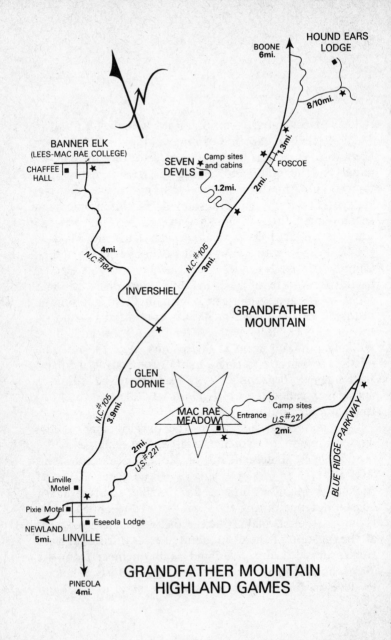

GRANDFATHER MOUNTAIN
HIGHLAND GAMES

in 1889 created the resort village of Linville. He was also responsible for the improvement of the Wrightsville and Carolina beaches near Wilmington and built what is now U.S. Highway 221 from Linville to Blowing Rock which he turned over to the federal government for one dollar. He also organised and financed great water power schemes in the state. After his death what remained of the original Linville Company was divided among members of his family, and today his daughter, Mrs. Agnes MacRae Morton and her family are building a sixteenth century Scottish village at Invershiel near Grandfather Mountain in the western highlands near Linville. Fourteen years ago, Mrs. Morton and her son Hugh helped in the promotion of the Grandfather Mountain Highland Games, to foster and restore interest in traditional dancing, piping, athletic achievement and Gaelic culture, and to create and establish scholarship funds to educate North American students of Scottish ancestry at Scottish universities.

In the Grandfather Mountain area is the Lees-MacRae college at Banner Elk. This college of Further Education, which gives a wide variety of· courses, was originally named the Elizabeth MacRae Institute, in memory of the wife of Alexander MacRae of Wilmington, N.C. Mrs. MacRae (1825-1907) became a pioneer in education in the state after the Civil War and with the financial assistance of Mrs. Lees of Georgia, set up an educational establishment at Banner Elk. From these small beginnings has developed the Lees–MacRae co-educational college of today, set in beautiful surroundings, 4,000 feet above sea level, providing accommodation and educational facilities in arts, science and medicine for nearly 1,000 students.

Many MacRaes, after landing at Wilmington, N.C.

moved inland and travelling up the Pee Dee River, established the little town of Sneedsboro. Unfortunately the court house of that town was burned during the Civil War and the records of dates, names and the places from which they came were destroyed. Some MacRaes, MacKinnons, MacInneses and Camerons later moved up country to the County of Anson and eventually settled at a place they called Morven, where their descendants are living today. According to Mrs. May who wrote a short history of the Presbyterian Church at Morven, one stained glass window in the Church was designed with the MacRae coat of arms, in memory of the MacRaes who were charter members.

A highway historical marker at Gautier, Mississippi, points out the grave of John MacRae, pioneer merchant and trader, whose son John J. MacRae became Governor of Mississippi from 1854 to 1858. John MacRae (senior) was a cotton buyer who put into operation the first barges on the Pascagoula River for shipping cotton to New Orleans.

After studying law, John J. MacRae was elected to the State Legislature where he was appointed Speaker of the House. This was followed by his election to Congress and then by his appointment to take the place of his friend Jefferson Davis in the U.S. Senate. After he was elected Governor of Mississippi his administration began the development of railways in the state and he was instrumental in having the Mobile and Ohio Railway built. Although he opposed secession in the U.S. Senate after his term of office as Governor, he resigned to go along with his state and was afterwards elected to the Confederate Senate where he served until the surrender of the South. Broken in health and fortune as a result of the war he took a trip, in 1868, to British Honduras to visit his brother Colin, who had been the agent for the Confederacy in Europe during the war. He died on his arrival and was buried at Belize in British Honduras.

One of President Davis' first official acts after the outbreak of the Civil War was to issue letters of marque, which amounted to licensing private vessels to be armed to make war on enemy shipping. One of these 'privateers' was the 'Confederate Steam Ship McRae', formerly called the 'Marquis de la Babana', purchased and renamed at New Orleans in 1861. The 'C.S.S.McRae', a sloop of 830 tons and carrying several guns was, according to the official records of the Union and Confederate Navies, sunk in the Mississippi River on 28th April, 1862.

On the banks of the Bucatunna, Wayne County, Mississippi, stands the trim little Philadelphus Presbyterian Church of which the family of Daniel and Margaret MacRae were founder members. They came from Sneedsboro, North Carolina with a family of six sons and four daughters. An entry in the old session records of the early church reads: July 31, 1831; 'On motion Mr. Graham was appointed to inquire of D. MacRae as to the truth of a report in circulation that he had permitted fiddling and dancing in his house on a certain occasion. Mr. Graham reported that Mr. MacRae acknowledged the truth of the report and promised with much tender contrition in future not to countenance or permit such practices in his house.' A survey of the membership roll of the Philadelphus Church from 1821 to 1950 shows that more than one third bore the surname MacRae, while in the cemetery adjoining the church seventy-five MacRaes lie buried.

Before the middle of the nineteenth century, families of MacRaes from the Carolinas moved south into

Georgia and Alabama where many of their descendants still live. Among the original settlers of Telfair County, Georgia, was Alexander Bain MacRae who was born in Scotland in October 1771. He went from N. Carolina to Georgia about the time that the area was being organised and received a grant from the State of Georgia of four lots of land (1815-1818). It is on this land that the town of McRae, Georgia, now stands.

In Montgomery County, Georgia, the Mount Vernon Presbyterian Church was founded and the first infant christened in that church was named Mary Melinda MacRae. One of the first four elected to the office of ruling elder, in 1851, was Duncan MacRae. A survey of church records shows that the MacRaes played a prominent part in the establishing of this church. It is also interesting to note that as early as 1855, coloured slaves were admitted into full membership.

Other members of the clan moved westward from the east coast and settled in Arkansas and Texas where land was cheap. A descendant of one of these migrants, Thomas C. MacRae, who was born in Union County, Arkansas, became Governor of that state in 1925. During his administration the Negroes were granted greater freedom and women were, for the first time, given the right to hold public office.

As a result of the defeat of the South in 1865, many of the settlers were impoverished and trekked further west to build new homes in Utah and California. John MacRae writing from Camden, South Carolina, to his brother Archibald in Britain stated: 'Our poor country is in a very impoverished condition. Credit is entirely destroyed. Money is at a usurious rate of interest and cannot be borrowed on real estate which has now only a nominal value.'

V

While their fellow clansmen were blazing trails across the American continent and suffering these hardships which have been more than adequately portrayed by Hollywood's film studios, the MacRaes who remained in Kintail were being subjected to ruthless changes in their mode of living. These changes are well described in a letter written by the Rev. Dr. Alexander Downie, who was minister of the neighbouring parish of Lochalsh from 1791 to 1820. 'When the valleys and higher ground were let to the shepherds, the whole population was drawn down to the seashore, where they were crowded on small lots of land to earn a subsistence by labour and by sea fishing, the latter so little congenial to their former habits. This cutting down of farms into lots was found so profitable to the proprietors that over the whole district, the sea coast where the sea is accessible is thickly studded with wretched cottages, crowded with starving inhabitants. Ancient respectable tenants, who passed the greater part of life in the enjoyment of abundance and in the exercise of hospitality and charity, possessing stock of ten, twenty and thirty breeding cows, with the usual proportion of other stock are now pining on one or two acres of bad land, with one or two starved cows; and for this accommodation a calculation is made that they must support their families and pay the rent of their lots. It is distressing to view the general poverty of this class of people aggravated by their once having enjoyed abundance and independence and we cannot sufficiently admire their meek and patient spirit, supported by the powerful influence of religious and moral principles.'

Driven from their homes in the glens of Kintail and

Lochalsh, during the first half of the nineteenth century, many were forced to emigrate to Canada. Some of the MacRaes who left settled in Nova Scotia. The following entry from a church record bears this out and illustrates the difficulty presented by Gaelic names to English scribes: 'This is to certify to all whom it may concern that Dunkin McCoy (Duncan MacKay) and Mary Mcraee (MacRae) have been lawfully joined together in the bonds of marriage by me Frederick David Basten of the Congregational Church in Manchester in the County of Sydney and Province of Nova Scotia, September 26th, 1822'. Some of the settlers, however, left from St. Ann's, Nova Scotia, with the Rev. Norman MacLeod on 28th October, 1851 in the 'Margaret', a barque of 236 tons and sailed for Adelaide, Australia. From there most of them were shipped to Waipu, North Island, New Zealand where they settled down and built a church. During the next few years, five other ships left Nova Scotia for the same destination. Among those who sailed on the 'Highland Lass', a brig of 179 tons, was Ann MacRae, widow of John MacKenzie and mother of Captains Duncan and Murdoch MacKenzie, ship owners of Baddeck, Nova Scotia. Mrs. MacKenzie died in New Zealand in 1871 at the age of ninety-three. Six years after the death of the Rev. Norman MacLeod, the Rev. William MacRae was inducted to the charge of Waipu and Whangarei Head. Although he was a capable man and won the support of the younger members of his congregation he could not take the place of MacLeod in the hearts of some of his elders. The result was that he resigned his charge in June 1883. Years later he was accidentally drowned in Sydney Harbour. Many MacRaes however remained in Nova Scotia and their descendants are still there speaking the Gaelic language of their ancestors. A son of one of

these emigrants, Milton A. MacRae who was born in
Detroit U.S.A. in 1858, became a journalist and helped
to establish the Scripps McRae League of newspapers.
He also wrote the book, *Forty Years in Newspaperdom*,
in which he states, 'My father, Duncan B. MacRae, came
as a wee lad to Canada, with my paternal grandparents
from their native heath in Kintail, Ross-shire.'

During a period of eighty years evictions and
emigration to Canada continued. Some, however, who
were driven from Kintail in the early part of the
nineteenth century settled in Lochalsh and Skye. The
sufferings endured by the families of John and Duncan
MacRae of Boreraig, Skye are described so adequately
by John Prebble in his excellent book, *The Highland
Clearances*, that it is unnecessary to add further detail.

As a result of the potato blight of 1846 and 1847
when the tubers rotted in the ground many people in
Kintail were destitute and further emigrations took place.
On 8th June, 1849, over one hundred people from the
parishes of Lochalsh and Kintail were shipped from
Balmacara to Greenock where they were put on board
the Circassian' which sailed from there to Montreal. On
this ship alone there were more than fifty MacRaes. For
the voyage each adult was given an allowance of seven
pounds of oatmeal and seven pounds of Indian meal per
fortnight and the total value of the meal supplied by
the Relief Board to the emigrants amounted to £43. 1s.
9d. It was calculated that the people could exist on this
meal until 30th September. The price of oatmeal then
was sixteen shillings per boll (140 lbs.) and Indian meal
thirteen shillings. According to John M. Gibbon who
wrote *Scots in Canada* there were 465 MacRaes in
Glengarry, Ontario by 1852. A group of these emigrants
settled in a hamlet which they named Kintail, on the

eastern shores of Lake Huron. With the development of the Western Provinces and the building of the Canadian Pacific Railway many moved westward and made their homes in British Columbia and the Yukon where there are today more than 1,000 MacRaes.

But Australia received her quota. Between 1852 and 1857 the Highlands and Islands Emigration Society was formed to help landowners ship away those who wished to emigrate to Australia. Again the majority of those who emigrated from Kintail and the adjoining parishes were MacRaes who sailed from Liverpool on the 'New Zealander', 'Priscilla' and 'Arabian' for South Australia and New South Wales. These long, arduous voyages were undertaken in conditions which beggar description.

From 1860 to 1920 emigrations continued and the number of MacRaes in Kintail is now so small that the prophecy of *Coinneach Odhar,* the Brahan Seer appears to have come true when he declared that he saw the day when all the MacRaes in Kintail could be shipped away in a small fishing vessel. So the final words of the song 'The Scattered Children of Kintail', written over 50 years ago by Kenneth A. MacRae, an exile, are charged with fresh poignancy:-

> 'But a silence dwells upon the land
> And broods in every glen
> And never shall we gather round,
> The ceilidh fires again.
> The red deer sleeps in sheltered nooks
> Where homes were wont to be
> And those who loved and laboured there
> Are exiled o'er the sea.

Though our restless feet have wandered far
And severed wide we be,
The children of a common stock,
A clan till death are we,
Yet the hills we loved shall ne'er resound
Our slogan's thrilling peal
Nor catch the tumult of our march
Come throbbing down Glen Shiel.'

Miscellaneous Clan Notes

Name

The surname MacRae presents problems of spelling. In the Scottish Highlands the recording of names was difficult because the native language was Gaelic and when English scribes attempted to write the Gaelic names corruptions resulted. The members of the Mac-Raes of Inverinate, within comparatively recent times adopted the spelling 'Macrae', presumably on the grounds that since the name was a personal one, which did not mean son of Rae, this spelling was the more correct. A study of the letters signed by Farquhar MacRae, Chamberlain of Kintail, who was the last of that family to hold the lands of Inverinate, shows that he always signed his name as Farq^r MacRa. (See Delvine Papers). And since the capital letter is used by other clansmen both in Scotland and elsewhere, the present spelling is adopted solely for uniformity. With the departure of MacRaes to distand lands further corruptions in spelling appeared. Where 'Mac' surnames were followed by a soft consonant or a vowel there was a tendency for scribes to add a capital 'C'. Thus MacAllister became McCallister, MacLeod became McCleod and MacRae, McCrae.

Clansman's Badge or Crest

The Clansman's badge on the cover of this book forms part of the Coat of Arms of Inverinate and this has been selected because it appears in *Tartans of the Clans & Families of Scotland* by Sir Thomas Innes of Learney, Emeritus Lord Lyon King of Arms. It should be added however that Sir Colin G. Macrae, W.S., representer of the House of Inverinate, who claimed arms as Chief of the Clan before the Lyon Court in 1909 had his claim challenged and disallowed.

The clan badge was the fir club-moss (lycopodium selago); Gaelic − *garbhag an t-sleibh*. The plant badge of a clansman was a sprig fixed on a staff, spear or bonnet. It was supposed to possess magical powers as the following translation from the Gaelic indicates:-

The fir club moss is on my person,
No harm or mishap can me befall,
No sprite shall slay me, no arrow shall wound me,
No fay or dun water nymph shall tear me.

The clan slogan or war cry was *'Scur Uran'*, the most prominent peak of the Five Sisters of Kintail (in the Parish of Glenshiel).

Coats of Arms

Macrae of Inverinate:

Argent, a fess azure between three mullets in chief and a lion rampant in base gules.
Crest: A cubit arm grasping a sword proper.
Motto: *Fortitudine* (By Fortitude)
　　　　　　　　　　　Lyon Register XXVII.

MacRae of Conchra:

Argent, a fess between two mullets in chief, and a lion rampant in base gules.
Crest: An arm in armour holding a scimitar proper.
Motto: *Fortitudine* Lyon Register XIX.

Clan Music

The MacRaes were noted exponents and composers of high-class pipe music. Among these were Finlay Dubh MacRae who composed several fine piobaireachds, Pipe Major Donald MacRae, a famous veteran of the 72nd. who won the prize pipe in 1791, his son Alexander, Pipe Major of the 71st and Pipe Major Farquhar MacRae,

Highland Light Infantry, who was, in 1913 responsible for the formation of the Clan MacRae Pipe Band. Between 1921 and the outbreak of the Second World War, this band had an unequalled record in Pipe Band contests.

Distinctive clan pipe music includes:

Failte Loch Duich (Loch Duich Salute).

Blar na Pairc (Gathering). This piobaireachd commemorates the victory at the Battle of the Park in 1491.

Spaidearachd MhicRath (The March of the MacRaes). This piobaireachd was composed in honour of 'Big Duncan of the Battleaxe' and of the deeds of his fellow clansmen in the Battle of the Park. The clan later adopted it as their march to battle. The composer is not known. *Cumha Dhonnchaidh Mhic Iain* (Duncan MacRae of Kintail's Lament). There are several versions of this old tune. One setting is noted by Donald MacKay in the Ballindalloch MS called Donald MacRae's Lament Inverinate, 1299.

Two songs associated with the MacRaes are:- *Theid mi dhachaidh Chro Chinn T-saile* (I shall go home to the Cro of Kintail) and *The Scattered Children of Kintail.* The former is a slow air and was often played on the bagpipes at burials in Clachan Duich Cemetery. There are at least two versions. One version was written by Dr. Farquhar MacRae but the other which is more popular is frequently sung in Gaelic on both radio and television. *The Scattered Children of Kintail* was written by Kenneth A. MacRae and always sung at clan gatherings by the Mod gold medallist, Kenneth J. MacRae.

Septs of the Clan MacRae
Macara MacCraw MacRaw Macra MacCrae Macgrath Macrath MacRaith Macrach MacCrea MacCrie Rae

The Black Chanter of Kintail is part of a black ebony set of bagpipes which was for several generations one of the heirlooms of the Seaforths. The chanter however is much older than the drones and is held together by seven engraved silver bands.

The stock of the big drone has the following inscription:-
'From Lord Seaforth, High Chief of Kintail to Lieutenant-Colonel Sir John MacRa, K.C.H. of Ardintoul, late of 79th Cameron Highlanders'.

The bagpipes are now the property of John MacRae of Eilean Donan Castle.

Eilean Donan Castle

This beautifully situated castle occupies the top of a small rocky island at the junction of Loch Duich, Loch Alsh and Loch Long. This situation is naturally strong and was likely to be selected at an early period for a fortress. It is supposed to have been occupied by a vitrified fort which was replaced early in the 13th century by a castle as a stronghold against the Norsemen. It gets its name from St. Donnan, who on Easter Day, 618, was killed, along with fifty-two monks, on the island of Eigg. In the fourteenth century the castle was in the hands of Randolph, Earl of Noray, who in 1331 adorned its walls with the heads of fifty victims as a warning to the inhabitants of the region. As Wyntoun says:-

> And the heidis of thaim all
> Were set up hie upon a wall
> Of a tour of Elandonan.

During the fifteenth and sixteenth centuries Eilean Donan was the chief stronghold of the MacKenzies of Kintail and in this period it was attacked on several occasions by Huntly and MacDonald of Sleat. It was finally blown up after the garrison surrendered on 10th May, 1719. For two hundred years it remained a picturesque ruin until in 1913 it was bought by Lt. Colonel John MacRae — Gilstrap who with the help of Farquhar MacRae of Avernish began the work of restoration. It was finally completed in 1932 and opened to the public.